“There are Sharks in

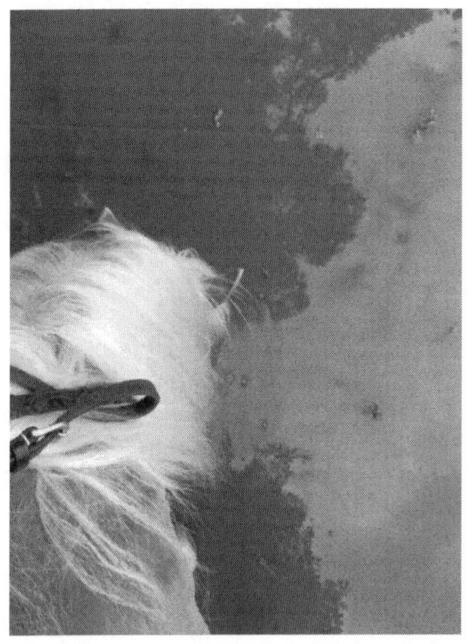

The 2016 collection of FP stories, guides to life as an FP and other little nuggets brought to you from my Facebook page.

Thank you Julie Holtom for coming up with such a cunning title! It's what I tell the Scottish Oik every day....

*

Thank you for choosing to travel on the FP Express non-stop service from field to valley and back again. We are expecting a great deal of turbulence on this occasion so you might be needing a seat belt and a stiff drink. Emergency exits are over the shoulders, between the ears or out the back door but I'd suggest a parachute as if you bail out, you WILL become airborne for a short while. We don't come equipped with sick bags either so use your helmet.

Are you sitting comfortably?

CHARGEEEEEEEEEEEEEEEEE.

*

Chapter List

Chapter 1: We've Broken The Human

Word of the week: Dehaffination.
The definition of being parted from ones Haflinger (whether on board or on the ground).

Today, the human was comprehensively Dehaffinated by an overenthusiastic, old enough to know better specimen who didn't really want to play the leading game and won by leaving at warp speed and pulling the human over in the mud.

coughs whoops....

*

We've broken the Human. Well, when I say "we" I mean SFP has managed what I've been striving to achieve for 14 and a bit years and the Human is now Plastered. No, not from gin – she was totally De-Haffinated at of all places, a dressage competition. A nice man in A&E gave her some silly gas and a plaster cast and she is now languishing in bed getting plastered in the more traditional sense seeming as she's now off work for a month.

*

Splat Day + 1: Human status: cross, ouchy, out of gin and in need of cuddles.

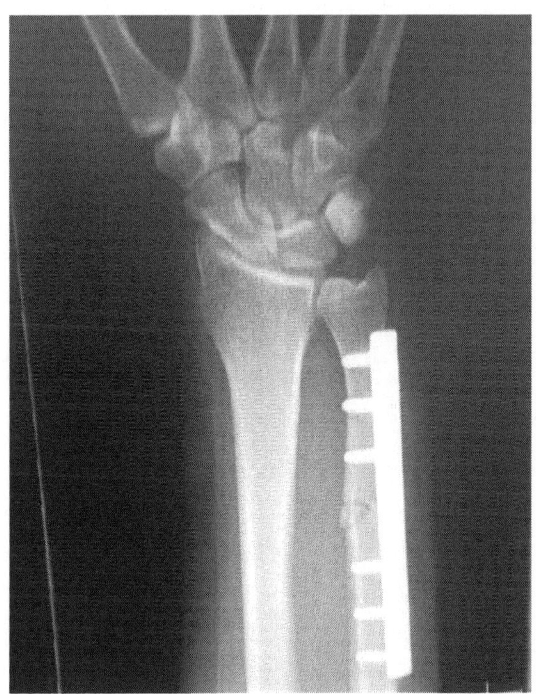

Splat Day + 2: The Human is going to the vet later to be screwed back together again and therefore is Nil by Mouth. This is such a horrifying thought that I am standing with her in solidarity as I too am hungry...

*

Splat Day + 3: Human status: home from the vet with a bionic arm full of metal, a load of happy pills and a gin ban. I think this is the cause of the groaning coming from her sick bed...

Splat Day + 4: The Human is itchy, which means she's healing. Or it could be the coating of ginger hair I left all over her as payment for a cuddle #moulting #LookLikeAYetiAlready

*

Was just enjoying the congratulatory pat from the human for being such a good pony for 4 days running when she noticed that I only had one shoe left on out of 4. I think the medication must have gone to her head however as all she did is chuckle and say it's a good job she loves me...

*

Managed a week of being good before it all ran out in one go. The one-armed bandit, errr I mean the human, appeared with buckets and was comprehensively mugged because it was late. Breakfast now covers a 100 metre radius and she has mud up her nose. I did try and apologise by licking her better but it just smeared the mud and resulted in declarations that I was "going to be made into a rug". Whoops.

*

Just watched the human take a full 10 minutes to shuffle down the hill with our breakfast. Progress was painfully slow and accompanied by WORDS and winces.
So what did we do when she finally arrived in our field?

Ooops....

So the human had to apologise to the Hospital Consultant this morning because I drooled on her bandage. Personally I can't see the issue with FP spit, I mean it could have healing properties and all that.
Or it could have just meant she had a green arm....

*

Laughing at the human as she has been researching anti-inflammatory remedies for her bionic arm and has raided my store of curry powder to mix herself up a potion. There are nasty choking sounds coming from the kitchen at the moment. Dearest Human, there is a reason why I don't eat it...!

*

In the paddock this evening:

Me: WHAT is this thing approaching?
SFP: It doesn't look very well.
Me: It's groaning. Do you think it's technically alive?
SFP: *gasp* Do you mean.... I ZOMBIE? Is this the Apocalypse?
Me: Quite possibly. I suggest a tactical retreat with lots of snorting.

It's the human. She's not only suffering from the annual Badminton Liquorice surfeit but she's also suffering because she'd tried to run it off. I keep telling her both liquorice AND exercise are bad for you *shakes head in despair*

Chapter 2: There Are Sharks in that Puddle: Training the Oik

Don't know whether to be proud of the Scottish Oik who let the human ride him for the first time ever and behaved impeccably, or exasperated that he paid absolutely no attention to my yells of advice over the fence and refused to buck her off. What's more, he came back with a mouth full of carrots and wouldn't share. Hmmm.

*

I spy SFP with the human on board waiting for his next carrot. He managed a wonky circle in walk today but steering is pretty much non-existent *grin*

*

"I won't ride the 4 year old" says the human. "It's too windy and he's doing laps of the field with his tail in the air, so it's too risky. I'll ride FP instead as he will be much more sensible in this weather."

Well, that was just asking for trouble wasn't it? She knows the wind makes me do handstands. THESE were particularly acrobatic *snigger*

Of course we're currently out of gin so the human is decanting some sort of horrible potato vodka she brought back from foreign climes which has been lurking at the back of the drinks cabinet for a good 10 years. I'm not expecting breakfast on time in the morning....

For the first time ever, the Human rode both of us today. I'll leave you to decide who was the good pony and who was so monumentally awkward that the human had to get off and pull....

*

So, SFP arrives back from his walk with a slightly wild expression in his eyes and a puffed out human in tow.
Me: What's wrong with you then?
SFP: Well, it was all going so well on our little plod then the human disappeared. I looked round for a bit and then something heavy landed in my saddle and asked me to walk on.
Me: And???
SFP: I galloped.

Ladies and gentlemen, my work here is done.

*

The Middle Sized Oik scrubs up quite well when he has to. He is off to learn stuff other than the things I teach him *smirk* #PonySchool

*

After searching all over the field for the SFP who appears to have gone AWOL, I resorted to standing at the top of the hill and wailing. This brought the human out with carrots and the explanation that SFP has gone to Pony School for a week and

I'm just going to have to man up without him to hold my hoof. This bad news was then cancelled out by the news that he has gone to Pony School with my saddle so I get the week off. RESULT.

*

Can be currently found looking over the gate into the black waiting for SFP to come
home #pining #utterlypathetic #needmorecarrots

*

Missing my Wing Man. Uprooting fence posts while the human is trying to re-do the paddocks is no fun by myself, even if it did make the human get all exasperated and threaten to shove me in the oven. Meanwhile, the Wing Man in question is rather bewildered to be having to do the work thing and spent most of the session shouting. #PonySchool

*

So, SFP has been home 6 hours, the fence is down and I've escaped for the first time in 2 weeks. I think this says everything you need to know about who is the naughty one at FP towers.
In all seriousness though, am super proud of the Scottish Oik who has graduated from #PonySchool with first class honours and won his first rosette at Dressage this morning after only 2 weeks under saddle. More importantly as he is now the

official FP Towers Dressage Pony, I never ever have to do dressage again. Oh yes.

*

This is fantastic. The human comes to the gate with a headcollar and the first pony to arrive at the gate gets ridden. Because SFP is a bit soppy about the human, he trundles off for what he thinks are cuddles and comes back looking exhausted about 40 minutes later. Meanwhile, I've perfected the art of hiding behind the trees and sleeping while he's gone. Perfect.

*

Ok, there's only so much of SFP coming back to the field smelling of carrots that I can bear.
This evening I was first at the gate and wouldn't let the human anywhere near SFP until I'd had a) at least 3 carrots, b) a cuddle and c) a promise that I am still the most awesome pony in the field.
SFP says I'm a complete sissy.

*

This morning: an unseemly tussle to be first to get nose into proffered headcollar and therefore receive carrots. After 5 minutes of wrestling in front of a bemused human, SFP won but I pulled out my trump card and absolutely refused to move from the gate so he couldn't get out. So the headcollar ended up on my nose instead *smug face*

Lovely hack and on my return, I gave my best Bambi eyes only to be met with the awful news that SFP ate the last of the carrots yesterday.

AAAARRRRRRGGGGGGHHHHHHH!

*

Today: SFP arrives back from manoeuvres looking positively steamy.

Me: Gosh SFP, you're looking a bit hot and bothered.
SFP: You didn't warn me about the lumpy brown and white things that go MOO. Hundreds of them! Nearly had me!
Me: Ah, THOSE. Zombie Cattle. They eat ponies you know. Especially Scottish ones.
SFP: Eeep. It's a good job I didn't let them get me.
Me: (knowing what's coming) This may explain why the Human is lurching in like John Wayne, straight to the gin cabinet. What DID you do?
SFP: I galloped.
Me: BRILLIANT.

*

Well, I may not have taught the Scottish Oik well with regards to behaving whilst being ridden in the arena (still saintly, blast him), but I can smugly report that he is now an absolute menace to catch. One sight of a headcollar and he turns into a squealy lunatic. You're welcome.

The moment has finally come. The human has said it's more fun to hack out SFP than it is to take me out. How RUDE. Apparently he doesn't argue about direction OR speed and just beetles along doing exactly what he's told.

HOW has 3 years of careful tuition come to this?? *sigh*

Ahhhhh, it's ok – I've just remembered the Nephew is coming on Friday. A fresh pupil to corrupt....

*

It's so much fun messing with SFP's mind. He hasn't quite forgiven me for telling him there was a Troll under the Countess of Thing's bridge (neither has the Human for that matter) so today's effort was a blinder.

SFP arrives home from another walk with a wild look in his eyes and an exhausted Human.
Me: And what happened this time?
SFP: *puffs* Huge Pink Snorty Things. MILLIONS of them.
Me: Ah THOSE.
SFP: They all came to the fence. I was nearly lunch, I'm sure.
Me: Well, I did tell you that Huge Pink Snorty Things like Haflingers for tea. But especially Scottish ones. What did you do?
SFP: I galloped.

Rumour has it the Human is threatening to put us in paddocks several miles apart....

So, the human had the splendid idea that she'd ride me and lead SFP to save going out twice. It was an idea that didn't really get airborne, or even off the runway for that matter. In fact, the idea pretty much exploded in the hangar when I decided I didn't want to drag the brat round the lanes and intimidated SFP so much, he refused to go anywhere near me and so the human couldn't even get us both out of the field. Then, while the human was consoling SFP and telling him I didn't really mean the death stare (I did), I took advantage of the slack reins and left the scene altogether. It took 15 minutes to catch me again by which time SFP had had a complete meltdown.

We got ridden separately.

*

Today, the Scottish Oik has been out doing the dressage thing and being revoltingly well behaved from start to finish. He even stayed clean from Wednesday's bath to Sunday which leads me to suspect he is not a proper FP.

My contribution to the day? Going to sleep in a dip in the paddock (muddy and full of pheasant poo) leading the Human to have a coronary at 5.45am this morning thinking I'd been stolen. Just as she was starting the sprint back to the phone, I surfaced, giving her another coronary and carefully cleaned the pheasant poo from my face by using her as a handy towel. I then beat her to the gate she had left open in her panic and made myself unavailable to be caught for approximately 4 hours.

THIS is how to be a proper FP. None of that mincing about in bling. The Oik is going to have to have remedial lessons *sigh*

This afternoon:
Me: Hello SFP. You've been a long time out on a plod. And WHAT is the brown groany thing at the end of your lead rope?
SFP: *coughs* We had a bit of an incident.
Me: Excellent. What sort of incident?
SFP: Well we went somewhere new. At the end of the somewhere new was an alligator pit. You know they like living in all that deep mud.
Me *gasp* What did you do?
SFP: Made the human get off and go in first.
Me: And then?

SFP: I jumped.
Me: *knowing the answer but wanting to hear it anyway* And where did you land?
SFP *proudly* On the human. It meant I didn't get eaten.
Me: And how many wellies did she lose getting out of the mud?
SFP: Two.

*

Me: Gosh SFP, you've been out with the human for ages.
SFP: We had a really long hack.
Me: *suspiciously* Were you GOOD?"
SFP: I think so. Thanks for the tip about the Sharks in the stream though. Didn't dare put a hoof in there just in case.
Me: Ahaaa. So what did you do?
SFP: Made the human go through first. She's still alive but she has wet feet now. #leakywellies
Me: And what did you do then?
SFP: Jumped. It made the human fall over in the mud.
Me: Outstanding work.

Corrupting innocent young minds is such fun *smirk*

*

Email from Granny:

Dear Arnie,
Now you are not to go into a bad mood, BUT, your Scottish friend has just won a competition for his good looks. I think

you should take all the credit for the way you have spent hours training him to make the best of himself in front of a camera. Make sure you are signed up as his manager and get a percentage of all his carrots.
Your loving Grandma.

Grandma is a genius. Where do I sign?

*

Dear Arnie,
I do not know if you have been told yet but you are going to be left on you ownios while that woman takes that interloper from Scotland off to the show that used to be your treat, except for the horrid ring with the roof. I'm just telling you so that you can demand a full photographic record, stills and moving pictures, of the whole thing so that you can see what they have been up to.
Love Grandma

Wait, WHAT????

*

My careful tuition since Sunday has paid off judging by the interesting shapes SFP was throwing round the arena this morning #buckaroo#canteriswaytoomucheffort

*

I fear I may have taught the Oik too much. On seeing the human approaching with a headcollar this morning, he started doing a set of fairly impressive aerobatics which ended up with him going splat and developing a limp. The headcollar ended up on my head instead and I swear I saw him smirking. I would say "phooey" but the heavens have just opened so I've escaped schooling for the time being....

*

I'm in trouble with the Human for telling SFP that dustbins have teeth. Several months of careful hacking on bin day has been undone by one with its mouth open. 20 minutes of the Macarena in the middle of the road followed by a flat refusal to go past it. The Human then made the critical error of getting off to shut its lid to show SFP that it was only a bin and wouldn't eat him. She dropped the lid and it went bang. I now have a squealy hysterical thing back at the field and SFP isn't much more coherent either....

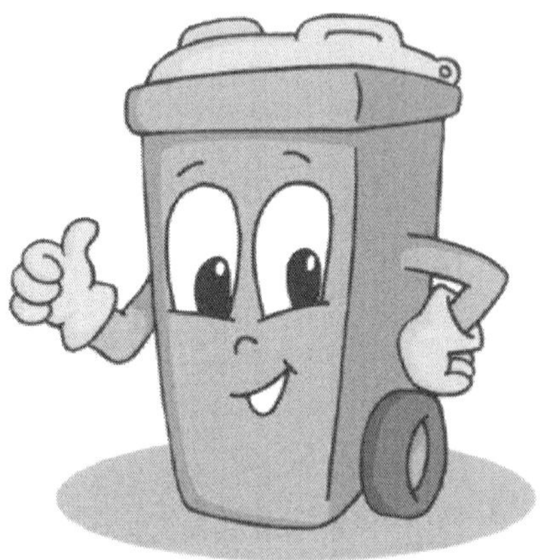

Chapter 3: What Fence?

Messing with SFP's mind is fun but messing with the human's is funnier. Thus, the human comes home from work to find us in the opposite paddocks to where she thought she left us this morning, with all fencing intact. Then while she is fetching hay, we swapped back. We're pretty sure the human is now thinking she's gone senile. Bahahaha.

*

Of course the neighbours haven't just had to email the human because I've just uprooted and unravelled several yards of fencing at the far end of the field.
And of course I'm not cross because I got found out. Can't have a party anywhere these days *sulks*

*

Two paddocks away from where I should have been this morning and all fencing intact.
Just call me The Ginger Ninja *smirk*

*

Hello Human! You might want to be more careful when arriving home at 1am and not coming out with tea.
We heard you.
And the splintering wood YOU heard at 6am was a food-deprived pair of Haflingers deciding we'd go up to the house to help ourselves as we just can't get the staff these days....

Hello Human. Yes, we have escaped. Yes, we are going to run around in an excited fashion while you try and lasso us. Ah, you've brought reinforcements. Hello Mrs Landlady. OK, we will go back in the correct paddock. Yes, we are all hooligans. Sorry.
Thus, we all meekly trailed back through the (SFP Shaped) hole in the fence and promised to behave. The human says she'll believe it when she sees it....

*

Today the Human has learned that post and rail really isn't any match for a midge-laden Haflinger. Well, it's itchy out here and it makes a brilliant scratching post with the added bonus of 2 hours of grass when it falls over while the Human is at work. She's now outside in a suit with a hammer, a mouthful of nails and a grump because the ice in her gin has melted and watered it down...

*

So, the human is at home today while the car is off sick, pretending to do her tax return but actually having a lazy and watching the scenery out of the window.
We are all meant to be in the valley field and there is another pony about half a mile away on the other side of the valley who we yodel to occasionally.
Today, there are two ponies on the other side of the valley. One is suspiciously Haflinger-shaped and is busy filling its face with as much grass as possible. It is too far to see which

one is guilty but it has got the human off the sofa pretty smartish *chuckles*

*

SFP has orchestrated his own “Leave” campaign and has left me all on my own. BREXIT? That’s the noise the fence made when I pushed it over to try and join him.

Yes, it is 4am. I’d tie the fence back together rather than try and coordinate yourself to bang in nails as you’re not very awake are you? Good bed hair by the way.

The Human is now running her own “Remain” campaign by staying in bed and not bringing us breakfast as apparently we don’t deserve it...

*

Me: I’m bored. And hungry. And wet.
SFP: Where’s the human?
Me: Still in bed, eating doughnuts and watching men in shorts on telly.
SFP: And we’re out here getting soggy with no food. RUDE!!!
Me: Time for action. All this rain has loosened the fence stakes nicely.
SFP *getting the idea quickly* Gosh, I AM itchy. Best have a scratch. A nice Haflinger backside should do it....

THRACKKKKK PARTY TIME!!!!!

For all of 10 minutes *grump*. You have to hand it to the human – she can get out of bed, into waterproofs, retrieve two rogue Haflingers, fix the fence and be back in bed in record time these days. She's had expert training though....

*

So, the Human decided to let us share a paddock for the day on the understanding that I was not to put holes in SFP and he wasn't to limbo under the bit of fence in the corner. I think you can see where this is going can't you?

Anyway, the human arrived home and retrieved a holey SFP from the adjacent paddock and attempted to put him back in the correct place. She didn't bargain on the following.

Me: Wherever SFP goes, I'm coming too.
Human: Nooooooooo, not through the gap.....
Me: Too late.
Human: How on earth did you fit through there?
Me: Magic. I am now going to be unavailable for catching for approximately 20 minutes. Is that burning dinner I can smell?
Human: You little Wotsit. I'll be right back.

20 minutes later...

Human: I have come armed with carrots. Nose in headcollar please. NO, NOT BOTH OF YOU.
Me: Elders and betters first *minor scrummage* ooooh Human, are you OK? You've got mud in your hair.
Human: Arghhhh, ARGHHHH. GET IN YOUR FIELD. Hooray,

finally ponies in their correct paddocks
SFP: You'd have thought eh? Race you to the electric unit! You lose *goes through fence*
Me: PARTY TIME. By the way, the cat has just eaten your pudding.

Another 20 minutes later and we are finally in our own fields and the electric is on. SFP is doing squealy laps of his side and I am sizing up the gap he made on his limbo expedition and wondering if I'll fit. The Human says we're not going to be allowed in together again until 2017.

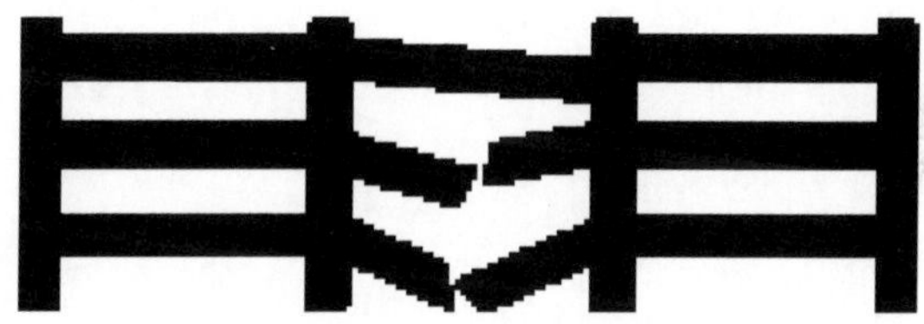

Chapter 4: Tis the Season to be Merry

Dear Father Christmas,
Some ramblers left the gate open. Honest.

*

So, for the first time in a while, it's not just FP smoochies the human will be getting for Christmas and therefore the human wants mistletoe. Having scoured the countryside for a suitable tree, she finds one in the corner of our field and arrives with a penknife.

First issue: it's a good 10 metres up. No problem says the human, I'll climb.
Second issue: the human is not 12 anymore and can barely get one leg in the first branch. Progress is woefully slow.

This is interesting viewing and I arrive at the bottom of the tree to watch. She is soon in the shape of a starfish and the language is getting colourful.

After a painful haul through the branches, the human reaches the mistletoe with a triumphant cry of "GOTCHA" and proceeds to try and hack a decent lump off the tree. The penknife is blunt and the language deteriorates further. Eventually, she has a handful which she lobs to the ground where it is immediately trodden on by yours truly. The human heaves an exasperated sigh and gets to work on a second gathering which she tucks into her belt and considers her route out of the tree.

It is now quite apparent that the human is stuck. Progress downwards is non-existent and instead she appears to just be climbing round the trunk in several directions. The audience now consists of me and the entire herd of Llamas in the next field and the language is now at basement level.

At this point, the human arrives at what she considered a genius solution.

Human: Ahaaaa, I have pony treats in my pocket *rattles the bag*
Me: Ahaaaaa, you have pony treats. Show me the pony treats.
Human: Just come and stand over here would you. My foot can just about reach your bottom and it would help me out of this tree if I could balance on you.
Me: Cough up a treat or two and I might consider it.
Human: Here you are, now just a fraction closer. That's it! DON'T MOVE.
Me: I won't. Keep the treats coming.

There is a noise like a bomb landing and SFP arrives at warp speed having heard the rattle of the treats, knocking me out of the way. The human, who has one leg on me and one leg still in the tree has no chance and there is a horrible cracking of branches and an even worse tearing of trousers noise. The human ends up in a splat shape in the mud and the treats cover a 50 metre radius while the mistletoe ends up in the Llamas' field and is immediately decimated.

I think the human is going to buy plastic mistletoe from the supermarket....

*

FP: caught first time and straight to the top of Father Christmas's good list.
SFP: caught second time but redeemed himself with bristly cuddles.
Obviously BFP knew something we didn't as it took the human an hour and a complete change of clothes to get her into the barn where the vet duly arrived and stuck needles in all of us.

I'm not being caught next time. It's worth the lack of Christmas Carrots just to avoid the needle *grump*

We're expecting a good descant for this one as the human has just had to unpick SFP from a prickly bush where I may or may not have shoved him...

♪♫♪ Hark, the Hungry Haffies Sing,
Speedily our munchies bring,
Hay on Earth and Christmas Treats,
Carrots for us all to eat.
Joyful all ye tummies filled,
Not a grain of breakfast spilled,
On the Human, who admits
Starving Ponies are the pits,
Hark, the Hungry Haffies Sing,
Glory to our Bucket King! ♪♫♪

Note to human: if you are going to feed us together, don't do it in sticky mud where you'll get your welly stuck and not be able to marshal the ensuing debacle. Of course nobody had their nose in the correct bucket by the end. The Nephew ended up with the pink bucket (Haaaaa) and I ate his carrots. The human? SOMEBODY pushed her over. As its nearly Father Christmas o'clock though, I'm not telling...

*

With 363 days to go until Father Christmas is next due, I suppose it was inevitable that somebody *coughs* misbehaved so badly that the human has spent the last hour repairing the Haflinger-shaped hole in the fence....

Chapter 5: Welcome Home Human!

The Human is home from yet another holiday. We were so pleased to see her that we forgot to be cross that she'd abandoned us and licked her all over. Mind you, I think she has finally learned that Airport Mints are a good investment...

*

Tonight: a slight miscalculation of gradient on realising the human was not only home from holiday but rattling a bucket of carrots at the opposite end of the field. The human was completely mown down by 4 joyful ponies and the carrots spread over a 200 metre radius. Whoops.
I suspect that the human didn't really miss us while she was away....

*

Hello Human! Did you have a nice business trip? Well, back to reality with a broken fence, a trashed summer paddock (it's the Oik's half though bahahaha) and two Haflingers who are not chestnut any more. You're going back to bed? Wise move...

*

And what's this lurching over the brow of the hill, clutching it's head and feebly waving carrots?
Apparently it's the Human. Are humans meant to be green?

This one is. Something to do with late night Guinness and Irish pubs apparently. Of course we completely mowed her down by way of a welcome home – you wouldn't expect anything less would you?

*

Hello Human, I see you're back. It's no good shining the torch out of the back door and counting eyes – I demand a cuddle. Aw, you're feeling sorry for me and have togged up to come and see me in this filthy weather. I am therefore going to lick you all over so enthusiastically that you fall over in the mud. Twice.

What do you mean you're going back to Austria on the next available flight?

*

Welcome home Human. Yes, we KNOW you're been unfaithful with Austrian stallions so we've staged an escape into the long grass *burps* where you have no chance of catching us. You'll use your belt as a headcollar? Nice idea but now your trousers have fallen down *giggle* and we're still hooning around like idiots. Of course you missed us....

*

The Human is going to look at Austrian Stallions again. We THINK she meant the 4-legged variety but she's got previous form on these trips....

Chapter 6: Fifty Shades of Brown

This evening: proof that the human doesn't need any help to fall over in the mud.

As she decided 7pm was a good time to put up some new electric fencing, we decided to keep our distance so we couldn't get the blame for ANYTHING. This was a good move as the language soon hit basement level when she dropped the torch in the mud and on retrieving it, went base over apex down the hill.

We're now forming a search party for a sock which didn't survive its visit to the bog....

*

SFP 1:0 Human who visited the mud face first and now looks like something from a zombie apocalypse *giggle*

*

Poor Human. She had to go back to the shed to mix us a 2nd breakfast after going base over apex in the snow this morning. Still, it means I get out of exercise as it is too slippery *happy face*

*

Rain makes mud slippery, especially at speed.

Just saying.....

*

Busy applying a layer of mud as the human has decreed it is dry enough for us to be rug-less all week. Note the lack of the word WARM. She may live to regret this decision when we start moaning fortissimo at 3am. Someone ring Ponyline please, my hooves are too cold to do anything...

*

Evening Cuddle with the human was hastily changed into an Evening Pat at Arms-Length, given that it's rained all day, brought all the clay to the surface nicely and I've rolled in it. SFP is so revolting he didn't even get a pat, just a heavy sigh *chuckles*

*

Bit of rain + no grass + steep gradient in field = slippery surface perfect for a good game of skittles. SFP is the ball and the human is the skittle. I gave him a good shove and got a strike first go *grin*

*

Hello Human. I see you've been to work and rather than change into wellies, have decided to wear inappropriate footwear to come and feed me. Silly Human, you know this is one of my favourite games....

SHOVE

I'm sure grass stains come out in a hot wash *grin*

You'd like to ride later? I'd say you'll need a chisel and a blow torch by then. And don't look at the Middle Sized Oik either. He's worse...

*

Laws of Haflinger Physics #1

You have 2 FPs. You rug one up overnight so it stays clean to ride in the morning. You leave the other naked.

Guess which one has now doubled in body weight through careful application of mud....

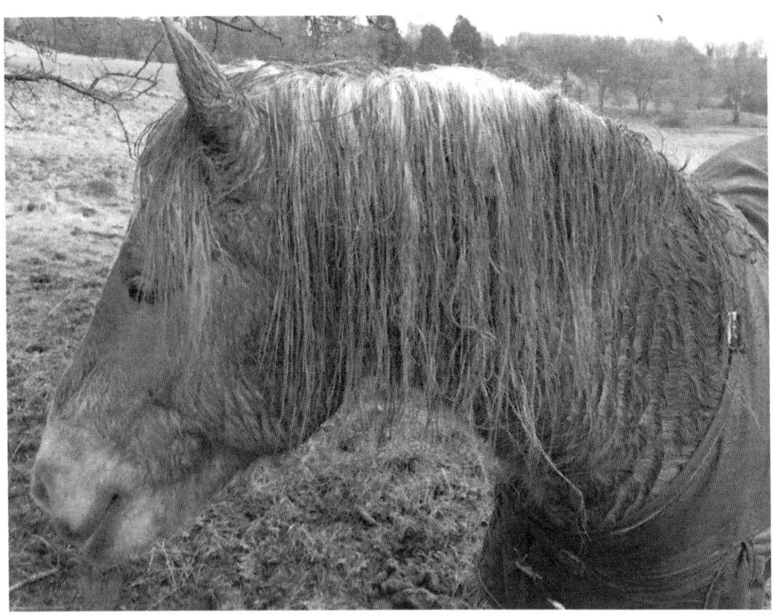

This morning in the field:

Me: Hello Human. Best of luck trying to find somewhere to pat me without getting a handful of mud.
Human: Ugh. I don't think I have enough brushes to even attempt a clean. You need the Fire Brigade.
Me: Sorry *grin*. So, I see you have a headcollar. The Oik is ready for you.
Human: It's your turn, dirt or not. Nose in please. Time you shifted a bit of flab.
Me: Flab is good insulation. Anyway, I've lost a shoe precisely to avoid this situation. It's HIS go *points hoof in direction of the 4 year old*
Human: He's had all his goes this week. And I have bad news for you, I have a hoof boot.
Me: Phooey.

A short time and a lot of straining later...

Me: Oh dear *happy face* the hoof boot doesn't fit. Cinderella is definitely not going to the ball.
Human: In case you had forgotten the fairytale, THAT makes you one of the Ugly Sisters.
Me: ...

What's worse, the Human then played her trump card. I got lunged. Triple Phooey.

Challenging SFP to a Mud Olympics. Whoever is the cleanest when the Human gets back from work gets ridden so this is a keenly fought contest#SundaysAreForSleeping

So, I was tied up and de-muddied. Of course I did what any true FP would do, shipped my headcollar and went for a roll. SFP is now claiming pony abuse as he has been ridden 3 days running. And the Human?

Gin

*

The loser of the dirtiest pony competition got to hack this evening. Annoyingly, said loser was revoltingly well behaved and again ate the last of the carrots. Maybe there is something in staying clean. Hmph.

*

Headlights at the opposite end of the field means the Human is visiting on her way back from work and thinks this is a cunning way not to get her work clothes dirty as it's not so muddy at this end.

Challenge accepted.

Oh my. I didn't even think it was possible to get that much soil in one human shoe....

Chapter 7: In search of fitness. I haven't found it yet...

So this morning I was a good pony and exercised the human, even though it was raining. Hopefully this will stop her developing any more stable vices and keep her looking lean and fit

*

Well, luckily for me, the timing of my increased workload has neatly coincided with the arrival of something called the Olympics. Which basically means the Human is going to be glued to the telly for the next fortnight. She claims to be enjoying the sport but I reckon it's really for the men in lycra.

Anyway, in honour of the XXXI Olympiad, SFP and I are trialling out a few sports of our own in the paddock thus:

100 metre sprint: Who can get to the proffered carrot first.

Skittles: Who can get to the proffered carrot first and knock the Human over.

Fencing: How many posts can be itched over in an hour.

Wrestling: Trying to avoid being slathered in fly cream. Bonus points for smearing it on any part of the Human.

Biathlon: A combination of eating and sleeping. Endurance is the key and points are lost for periods where neither of these are taking place.

Skiing: Taking the Human either downhill or slalom at the end of a lead rope.

Triple Jump: The number of fences to be cleared between mud and long grass

Squash: How many pink buckets have to be replaced after meal times.

Weightlifting: Who can carry the Human the furthest after she's been at the trifle.

*

What do you mean, I can't go for a gallop with the nice brown racehorse? *sulks* in that case, I am going to shift into donkey mode and watch you go all red in the face trying to get me to move faster than an amble.
SFP is better behaved? Hmph...

*

Lunged and schooled perfectly this afternoon and kept my halo intact for the entire hour. Canters on the bit and everything! Do I get any praise? Do I phooey – instead I got a thermometer shoved somewhere extremely personal as the human was worried I was sickening for something. I'm perfectly OK, it was just too hot to bother being naughty. Normal service will be resumed when I'm taken out and it's not BOILING. Sheesh....

Today I have been held up as a shining example of how a native breed should be managed weight wise by the local Vet who wants to take pictures of us to use in her lectures about pony diets. This is all very well and good but now I can't even TRY to petition for more food as the Vet says I don't need any *wails* and I'm perfect as I am. What's more, the Human has just gleefully told me I'm off to Boot Camp in 3 weeks for a toning session.

Help.

*

Hello Human. I see you have tack. You appear to be forgetting something though – it's 8pm and I've gone to bed with my haynet. What do you mean we're going for a Midsummer's Ride? I'M IN BED.
Well, if you are going to make me do this ride, I am going to do it at the slowest possible speed whilst still maintaining a forward trajectory. You're going to let SFP into my paddock to eat my haynet while I'm gone?
GALLOP.

I hate it when the human is all smug.....

*

So, gold star and top of the class on my first day's schooling at Boot Camp. Meanwhile at home, SFP has broken two bits of rail, uprooted one fence post and ended up with a fat ankle and on medication because he went splat whilst trying to jump out. Not to mention the incessant yodelling because he is in lurve with a GIRL next door. Honestly, I leave him 5 minutes....

*

FP 1:1 Human.

A very tired human came to ride and assuming I'd be exhausted from all my exertions at boot camp, expected a quiet ride.

Nope. 1 hour of loony.

However, on returning to barracks, I was handed over to the boot camp instructor and made to work the loony out in the school. This was definitely pony abuse.

NOW I'm tired....

*

Schooling? NOW? You are having a laugh surely. I'M IN BED.

Phooey. No peace around here any more....

*

Out on manoeuvres with the Human this morning and I punt off up the drive at approximately Mach 2. There are squeaks from above which I ignore until we finally have to stop to do a gate.

Human: OI!!! I only took you out because I was expecting a beach donkey, not a racehorse. This is only our 3rd ride this year and you're meant to be unfit and slow. What on earth is the matter?
Me: *Sniffs the air expectantly* I smell a pony party. Therefore I shall gallop until I find it.
Human: You oaf. That was YESTERDAY when the hunt came through.
Me: No matter. I can still smell other ponies so I shall still gallop. Best you fasten your seatbelt. CHARGEEEEE.
Human: *squeak squeak squeak squeak*

And we're home in a record time of 40 minutes. Result.

*

Post Breed Show and the Oik finally shows his face back at home. Much to my disgust, he actually won something so his head was almost too big to fit through the field gate but I let him in when he told me he ran away in the class where the human had to wear a big skirt as that must have been hilarious.

There's only one drawback to his return though – apparently he is having a month off. As the human still wants to ride, I have a nasty feeling my little period of lazy may be at an end. The Human has even mentioned the D word and it's not Dinner.

Help.

We're sorry we didn't have the headcam this morning as my first ride in 2 months produced a set of FP aerobatics that procured a round of applause from the farmers in the valley and a lot of squeaking from the Human.
Apparently I have a lot of F to shift. Hmph.

*

No, I'm not stopping to pose by the bluebells. I'm going to gallop. What do you mean I'm not allowed to gallop yet?

Whatever.

*engages warp speed *

Several fields and lots of squeaking later: You ok up there Human? Contemplating the gin cabinet are we? See, I got you there much quicker than if we stopped to take photos of sissy flowers...

*

Today's aim: to move as slowly as possible whilst still maintaining a forward trajectory. The 4 minute dressage test was stretched out to at least 12 minutes with a poo break in the middle. I think the Human remembers why she doesn't take me in the school very often. She has a stitch and has gone all purple. I've barely broken a sweat *grin*

Human: Hack time!
Me: errrr? I haven't just got one shoe missing – I've got 4 missing and I KNOW you don't possess 4 hoof boots.
Human: Don't be a sissy, it's only a short one and the road isn't stony.
Me: I'll moan...
Human: I'll ignore you.

So out we went and I grumped all the way until hoof hit carefully manicured turf.

GALLOPPPPPPP!!!!

And then didn't stop all the way home *smirk*

There is a postscript to this. Having also ridden the Oik this morning, the neighbours asked the Human if we were very different.

Oh yes said the human. One is like piloting a speedboat. Small, fast, light and very manoeuvrable. The other is like piloting a supertanker. Long, heavy, not very easy to turn and takes about a mile to stop....

*

The Scottish Oik and I have come to an agreement. Whoever is ridden first has to wear out the Human as much as possible so the second pony has a nice easy time. Thus I obliged this morning by delivering a wobbly-legged Human with a face like it had been in a wind tunnel to the field gate, only for her to declare she was too exhausted to ride SFP and needed to go and lie down. This was not quite how it was meant to work – he is looking unbearably smug and I'VE had to go and lie down...

*

Busy morning proving to the human that I am still #1 pony and way cooler than the Scottish Oik. Of course handstands are much more entertaining than just doing as one's told!

*

So, the Human put on her brave trousers today and decided to ride and lead for the first time ever. Because she has SOME sense and wanted to avoid complete carnage, she rode yours truly and led the Scottish Oik. However, it was not all plain sailing as the Oik took full advantage and bit me on my neck all the way round. Because I am a GOOD PONY, I did not retaliate. Worse news, the Human was so delighted with how we behaved that this is now going to be a regular occurrence. I will have to plot my revenge...

*

Bunged up nose? Blocked sinuses? Throw away those silly medicines and let the FP Blatomatic clear your head. Available in three settings – light blat, medium blat and warp speed depending on the severity of your condition.

Today, a medium blat for the tail end of the Human's cold.

Out on manoeuvres this morning: Can't be bothered, can't be bothered, can't be bothered, can't be bothered, oooo look, a new log to jump. CHARGEEEEE.

The human now looks as if she has been in a wind tunnel *snigger*

*

Busy evening showing the Human that I am way cooler than the Scottish Oik by hurdling every log in sight at full blat. Yes, the Human has tottered off in search of the gin cabinet but yes, she does have a huge smile on her face

#ItsMoreFunOnFP #NextStopBadminton

*

Oooo a 15 mile pony party. With another FP! And jumpies! This is FUN.

I'm not sure the human thinks so after 4 hours of loony. Someone come and help her out of the saddle...

*

The moral of this morning's hack is don't chicken out of a fairly sizeable jump when your FP has already got missile lock on it. I jumped it fine. The human on the other hand, went splat in the saddle and one of my ears went up her nose. Dignified? I think not *snort*

Well, it's finally happened. After this morning's debacle in the school (can't move, won't move), the human has decided that I'm never ever doing a dressage test again.

Result.

P.S. It does concern me that the Oik was hoof perfect though. 4 and a bit years of careful tuition have amounted to absolutely nothing. He's even stopped doing handstands on the lunge *sigh*

*

In the arena this morning:

Human: Trot on!

Me: No.

Human: We're not doing Dressage, I promise.

Me: Any movement in an arena is Dressage. I'm not budging from my nice slow amble.

Human: Pretty please?

Me: NO.

Human: But there's a jump in the cor.....WHOAAAAAAAA

Me: CHARGEEEEEEEEEEEEE.

Chapter 8: A FP Guide to the Show Ring

As every FP knows, there are several jobs one can have, and some of the more talented of us (looks smug) can succeed in more than one discipline. Yes, I KNOW Dressage isn't one of those successful disciplines here at FP Towers but that's now the Scottish Oik's job.

However, one of my jobs has been to parade round a show ring and win stuff by looking handsome. You'd think in my case, this would be easy but the Show Ring is full of strange rules and regulations and it's easy to get it wrong. Thus, here is my handy guide to all matters showing:

1. Enter the correct class. Not as easy as it might sound. Several years ago, an inexperienced Human stuffed me in every class going at a local show thinking it would be good for me. I don't think the carefully plaited brown ponies in the Ladies Hack class thought so, especially during the group canter when I delighted in thundering up their backsides with my ears back. We were asked to leave.
2. Be nice to the Ring Steward. If you get a Tweedy one, don't eat it. They are chewy and definitely not worth the effort. We were asked to leave.
3. Going round with everyone else: Throw intimidating stares at all the other ponies. If it's a ridden class, overtake everyone with your ears back and try and squash as much of the opposition as you can. Bonus

points if you make one squeal. We were asked to leave.

4. When one is presented to the Judge, don't decide that a) you need a wee, b) you need an itch and the Judge is the best itchy post or c) the Judge looks tasty (I refer to the previous point about tweed). Stand still, don't fidget and definitely don't roll your eyes when they ask "What is it?" We were asked to leave.
5. When the Judge asks you to walk away and trot back, the Judge is not a target to be mown down, no matter how many times you've practised Skittles with the Human in the field. We were asked to leave.
6. An individual show is the ideal time to show everyone else the interesting shapes you can throw in walk, trot and canter. Gallop is the best one though. Get asked to do that and your Human might as well throw in the towel. My record is 5 bucks and 2 leaps down one long side. We were asked.... oh never mind, you get the picture.
7. If by some miracle, after all of the above, you are still in the ring, still behaving and actually doing OK, there is a chance you might be placed. If this doesn't happen often, be prepared for your Human to cry. Mine is worse than a leaky tap in the show ring and blubs at even a minor placing.
8. If you get a rosette, it may be attached to your bridle which is the spookiest thing since the bin men left a bag in the hedge. After a few instances of near death

experiences the Human is wise to this now and has the rosette put on her number tie.

9. If you WIN, then soak up the adoration, lick the Judge and try not to dent the Trophy.
10. The Lap of Honour aka The Mass Blat. EVERY PONY FOR ITSELF. If you haven't won, make sure you overtake the winner and throw as many shapes as you possibly can. If you have won, you'll be in front. Go as fast as you can and see how many of the other ponies lose all braking systems. Don't let anyone overtake. You'll get more applause, honest...
11. Bonus Round: The Championships. For Goodness Sakes, BEHAVE. It's just not worth the aggro if you don't and Championships mean a LOT of extra carrots for being a good pony.

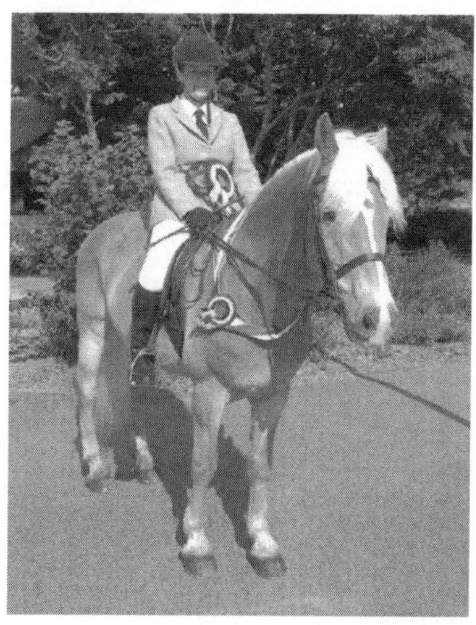

Chapter 9: Don’t look at the Clock...

Noisily petitioning for breakfast only for the human to open her bedroom window and shout something about clocks going back. But I’m HUNGRY.

*

MUMMY?!

Oh woe is meeeee, SFP has escaped and I'm all alone in the fog with nobody to hold my hoof. And I'm hungry.

MUMMMMMMYYYYY!!!!

Ah, there you are. Please go and retrieve the Limbo Master and rustle up breakfast while you're there. Yes, it is *technically* morning and therefore we can be fed. Good bed hair by the way. No, don't look at the clock, it doesn't begin with a 5. You did. What do you mean, breakfast isn't due for 3 hours and you're going back to bed? Hello SFP, nice of you to turn up. Did you hear the no breakfast thing? You did? Let us commence the noise.

MUMMMMMMMYYYYYYYY....

Surprising how quickly food turns up when the human is trying to keep on the right side of the neighbours.

Last morning of being fed in the dark until the new year. Shame really, as ambushing the human because her night vision isn't great is such a fun game. This morning's effort: 10/10 to SFP for the sneak attack and an A+ to me for finding all the carrots that fell out of her pockets.

*

Dear Human,
Getting up at 3.30am and switching the light on to make a cup of tea was never going to end well was it? We saw you #hungryyellsfortwohoursandcounting

*

Bets now being taken as to which pony, out of 2 FPs and an elderly grey job, has learned how to unpick rope and undo the gate into the next field. The Human was thus woken at stupid o'clock by a full on pony party.
The smart money is in the Scottish camp, as he has Previous in this crime, but we all got yelled at...

*

Breakfast at 7.30am followed by a doze. When I woke up, it was dark again, all the birds were asleep and SFP was also flat out and snoring. Therefore, once the sun re-emerged I think it was perfectly reasonable to noisily petition for breakfast again in the hope that the human thought it might be Saturday. What do you mean "NO"? And what's a Solar Eclipse?!!!!

So, after a well-executed escape last night, we have been put in our teeny tiny summer paddocks to deflate with teeny tiny miniscule holed haynets. I am sulking because SFP is in the side with a bit of grass which I thought was mine, and I am in the side we stripped bare last week when the fence blew over.

On the plus side, the Human's pit is now within yodelling distance. I predict a noisy rebellion at 2am, 4am and 6am. Ahem.

*

6.30am and the Human lurches out the back door wearing her pink fluffy dressing gown and wellies. She has not yet had her coffee. The torch beam flickers up and down the valley, finally alighting on 3 pairs of guilty looking eyes somewhere where they shouldn't have been.

Me: Morning. As you can see, we played paddock chess in the night and achieved checkmate.
Human: Argghhhh.
Me: Henry blew the fence over, honest.
Human: Arghhhhhhhhh.
Me: We've been in the long grass all night.
Human: ARGHHHH.
Me: You might not want to look at your hay pile either. It's errr, not as neat as it used to be.
(At this point, SFP tries to stand in front of it to hide the fact it looks like there has been an explosion)

Chapter 10: The Good just ran out...

So, as SFP is the master barrow tipper round here, the full barrow was left in my half of the paddock while the human went to get hay, with the threat "touch this and you'll be made into a rug."

Coming soon to Axminster Carpets, the "FP." Deep pile and quite thick (how RUDE). Not only did I tip the wheelbarrow over but I then jumped on it. It's not looking very well. Neither is the human for that matter who is looking dolefully at a gin bottle because even she knows that 7.30am is a bit early to start...

*

One of the most fun things about living here is the knowledge that if someone doesn't shut the bottom gate properly, there's always a chance that we get visitors from the slightly odd farm down the valley (hence the Large Beaky Thing who appeared in the last book).
Thus, this morning, a bleary-eyed human was met with a breakfast queue that consisted of 2 x Haflingers, 2 x Shetlands, 2 x Sheep and a Llama #needsmorebuckets

*

Today I have been a super good pony and had my pegs done without sleepy juice. The Oik meanwhile, DID have to have sleepy juice which means a) he also got clipped while he was dozing, b) I got his carrots and c) he's all wobbly which is a good game.

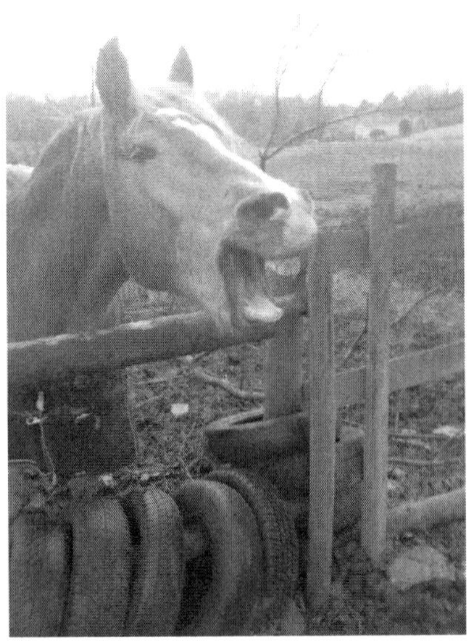

FP 1:0 Electricity Man up pylon. I suspect this postcode is going to have a warning put in the book about nosey ponies....

*

On surfacing this morning, the human was presented with a pony (SFP) who pretty much had more hole than rug and is claiming he's cold and wet. Seeming as the rug was brand new last Autumn, this has not gone down too well, especially when the reason for the gigantic holes became apparent. Well, the tearing sound is quite entertaining, especially if I pull really hard....

New game: helping the human fill water buckets from the stream in order to soak hay (SFP has a cough).

When I say helping.....

*

Dear Nice Tweedy Ramblers,

Taking the lid off your tupperware to triumphantly show us how many blackberries you'd picked on your 3 hour hike really wasn't the best plan was it? The suction power of a hungry Haflinger can hoover EVERYTHING within a 2 metre radius, including about 4lbs of carefully procured fruit.

Sorry...

*

It turns out SFP is having his photo taken next week and so has been put on an immediate and strict diet as his week off has done his waistline no favours.
Why then, have I also been put on the same diet when I'm not going anywhere near a camera? *wails*

ITS NOT FAIRRRRRR.....

*

What's this lurching down the field towards us? It's a bicycle. Atop which is a VERY wobbly Human. Apparently we are getting meals on wheels while she trains for something called a Triathlon.

Except we didn't get meals on wheels as she really hasn't got the idea at all, fell off (not pushed, before you all point accusing fingers) and landed on our breakfasts which were immediately hoovered up by the Elderly Grey Job.

sigh It's going to be a long winter....

*

Apparently, after 17 and 3/4 years on this mortal coil, it is now time to "man up." This means, according to the Human, that I'm not getting a rug on until she can see her breath, rain or shine and I have plenty of fat (how RUDE) to insulate me until then. Plus something about it being better for me to go Au Naturel?!!

The Oik meanwhile, has had his raincoat put on and has an insufferably smug look on his face. It's now tipping it down. I'm thinking that if I make enough noise, the human will eventually give in. All together now: OH WOEEEEE IS MEEEEEE.

*

Had to watch the terrible sight of my breakfast being blown out of its bucket before I'd even got my nose in it this morning and the even more horrible sight of a human with mad bed hair having to turn back and get a second helping. It's a smidge windy out here #TypicalBritishSummerTime

*

Hello Human. You're walking a bit funny. Been out for lunch you say? Quadruple helpings of lasagne followed by 3 puddings all washed down with a bottle of wine? Let me help you digest all that with a fine set of FP Aerobatics and the kind of gallop that induces turbulence and the need for a seat belt.
Feeling better? What do you mean, no???

*

Dear Human,
It's no good tiptoeing out on your patio to partake in a sneaky G&T in the hope that we won't spot you. We KNOW you're out there. Now for goodness sakes come and feed us before the neighbours serve us with a noise abatement order.

*

Bored of being hairy and shed my winter coat in one go all over the Human who only wanted a cuddle, not a ginger beard...

*

Killed the rug completely in the night. Now regretting it as the new one won't arrive until Friday. Meanwhile I won't let the Human put my fly mask on so she's let me in with the Oik so he can be my fly swat. He however, has other ideas #itchy

*

So, the new rugs arrived. The neighbour says it looks like we're in some sort of witness protection scheme for Haflingers and the view from their house now looks like the Serengeti...

A small amount of rain has produced a rare Brown Zebra. As this rug was new yesterday, this has not gone down at all well. Better than SFP though – his already has a hole in it...

This afternoon, alerted from my slumber by SFP making choking noises in the adjacent paddock:

Me: What's this? Wormer? No thanks - I think you'll find I'm unavailable to be caught *canters off at full speed*
Human: Well, SFP had his. Shall he have your carrot ration too?
Me: Yup. No wormer for me - I am going to now do handstands all over the paddock. Best of luck.
Human: *develops an evil grin* I have Christmas Mints...
Me: I'm right here. Show me the mints.
Human: Open wide.... And IN goes the wormer. 1:0 to me.
Me: SPITTTTTTTT. Oh dear *happy face* you seem to be wearing most of my wormer. Bit inadvisable to be wearing your work clothes don't you think? 1:0 to ME.
Human: I bought an extra dose just for this eventuality. Open wide.
Me: Mphhhhh. Nope.
Human: Pleeeeease *starts wedging mints into the corner of my mouth, then rams syringe #2 in*
Me: SPITTTTTTTTTTTT. You'll be needing a bath before you go back to work now as well.
Human: *wiping wormer from round her ear* Have the Alpacas next door been teaching you how to spit? You complete Hooligan.
Me: I love you Human. Have a smeary kiss just to make up for it. Good hair by the way.
Human: ......

There have been a lot of WORDS issuing forth from the Human's window this evening. With a big show on Sunday (thankfully it's the Oik's turn for a 6am cold bath, not mine), after 4 hours of turning the house upside down the Human has realised that the reason she can't find the smart leather lead rein for her in hand get up is because I ate it last year.

It was chewy and definitely not worth the effort.

*

Gone feral because the human is busy. Mugged the pony sitter, trashed my paddock and sat on SFP.

Being feral is fun...

*

Teamwork. I help SFP out of his fly mask and he helps me out of my paddock.

Sharing a field again has been put back to 2018.

*

Tonight, one of the trees in our paddock has eyes and a meow. Thus, we can be found boggle eyed and snorty at the other end of the field. This is however, until the Human rattles cat food at it...

#AllPetTreatsSoundTheSame #Chargeeeeee #HumanNeedsA BathAgain

Busy day making SFP's rug into what can only be described as a "convertible" meaning that it is now Topless.

It’s currently snowing. I'm not popular....

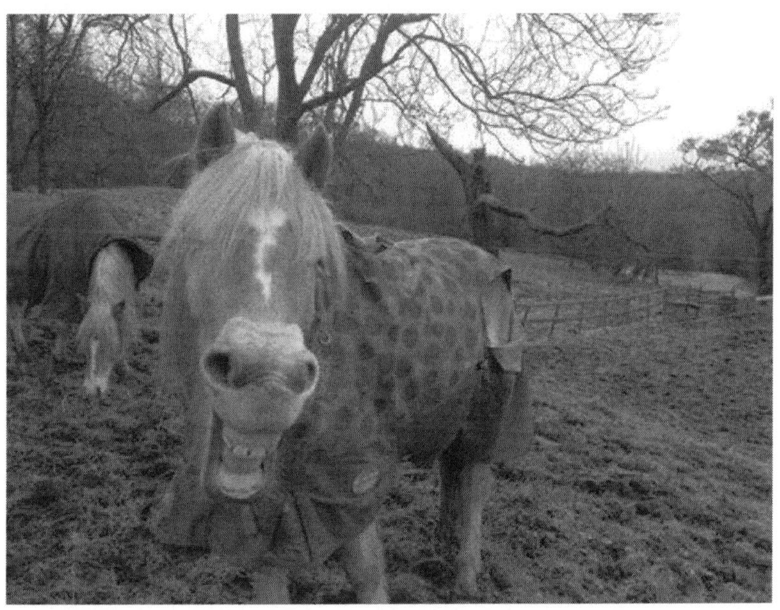

Well, the votes are in and have been counted and it's FP for Prime Minister again. Mainly because there were only two votes, mine and SFP's and I gave him the death stare until he gave in.

Please don't let him grow bigger than me....

Breaking News: Rioting overnight in the Constituency of Starvation Paddock & Valley when SFP demanded a recount. Damage included an overturned wheelbarrow and a dented poo scooper. Rioting was quelled by the 6am arrival of what can only be described as a THING with bed hair and a grump who immediately annulled the election result and declared a dictatorship as she had the keys to the feed shed.
Phooey.

*

Bike....

Bike, Bike....

Bike, Bike, Bike, Bike, Bike, Bike, SFP, Bike, Bike, Bike Bike, Broken Fence, Chaos, WORDS, Bike, Bike, Bike, Bike....

I think the local cycling club may be re-routing this particular ride next time *grin*

*

Well hello teenage tantrums and huge strops from the Middle Sized Oik who definitely DIDN'T want to cooperate in any shape or form today. He is not talking to the human now or me for that matter as it was my fault he ended up in the arena instead of me (lost shoe). Still, every cloud and all that #afternoonsnooze

I suppose those of you with small children will know that silence is ominous and usually means trouble.

The chorus of wailing from the diet patch that is the usual accompaniment to the hours of dusk suddenly abated. The Human's suspicions were justified by the sight of a Haflinger-sized hole in the post and rail, one happy Haflinger in knee deep grass and the other raiding the feed bin for the Elderly Grey Job.

Rumbled. Phooey.

*

Waited until I heard the distant *ponk* of cork exiting bottle before staging a cunning and dastardly escape plan. Sadly, the human was on the patio pouring the wine at the time and witnessed the whole debacle from me clearing the fence into SFP's paddock to realising that SFP's paddock is also devoid of food and therefore pinning the blame firmly on him and duffing him up.
Yes, I AM a hooligan and no I am not going to be on Father Christmas's present list this year. I REGRET NOTHING muhahahahaha.

*

First sun block of the summer applied to delicate pink nose, first hoof pointed in mirth by a chuckling Middle Sized Oik (who is not in possession of any pink bits) and sadly, first time he has won the ensuing fisticuffs.

We are both united however, in hysterical laughter over the human who neglected to sun-block herself and then fell asleep on her hammock. Medium to Well Done does not even come close to describing the level of cooking she received. Bahahahaha.

*

Celebrating being turned out in the winter paddock by hiding in the valley and giving the human a coronary every morning. And then giving her a coronary every evening as well with well-planned ambushes. Of course we're not utter hooligans....

*

Human 0:1 slippery wellies, steep gradient and full wheelbarrow.

I'd keep her down wind until she's had a bath...

*

Rather a shock after several weeks of lazy to overhear the human announce to the farrier that she had "8 weeks to whip Fatso's backside into shape, starting NOW with hill work." What on earth do I have to be whipped into shape for???

Errrr, help????

Lulled the Human into a false sense of security by letting her win our first Lun-Ging match in 6 months and being a super good, compliant and obedient pony.

SFP on the other hand won his match with a record score after staging a sit-down protest and then eating the lunge line. Brilliant.

*

FP 1:0 National Trust tea shop. Refused to leave until they had dispensed mints, drooled all over the cake counter and licked a nice lady in an apron. Today was a good day

*

The cunning and dastardly escape into the long grass worked right up until I was made to canter for an hour to deflate. Phooey.

*

The only problem with having a fit human is that she is far more stickable these days. I put in the whole range of FP aerobatics today and all I got was a chuckle from above. And this was bareback too. Time to prime the Middle Sized Scottish one methinks....

*

Hello Sheep. And your friend. And some lambs. And another sheep. And another....

Ok, that’s MY haynet. GET OFF. You’ve bought back up? More sheep?

MUMMYYY!!!!!

Current sheep head count is about 100 and my haynet has disappeared. Help?

*

Hot Air Balloon 1:0 Me. There I was, minding my own business out on a plod with the human when we rounded a corner and there was a HUGE stripey thing landing in the middle of my gallop field with some cheerily waving humans beneath. Of course it was the human who came off the worst with a face full of tree as I made my escape. Now we're home I think she may have actually climbed INTO the gin cabinet and shut the door....

*

Out on a plod today.

Me: *applies handbrake drastically and without warning* What is THAT??
Human: *peels herself up from between my ears* It's a dustbin you oaf. Why the sudden stop? You've already been past about 20 as its bin day.
Me: THIS one has its mouth open.
Human: Oh for heaven’s sake. You've had 14 years of bin desensitisation. Go over and sniff it and you'll see it's just the

same as the others. The bin men must have left the lid open.
Me: No. It's gaping at me and it WILL eat me.
Human *sigh* go ON. It won't hurt you.
Me: Ok, I'm approaching with extreme caution here. You could fit a whole FP in there and I'd rather not be lunched.
Human: Pathetic. Go on, put your nose in. See? SEE?

At this moment the lid closes on my head.

Me: ARGHHHH. It's eating me! KILL IT DEAD!!!
Human: Noooooo!

Grunch

Me: *looks at overturned bin with hoof print in lid* Did I win? Is it dead?
Human: We are not going out on bin day ever again.

*

No, the distant rumbling you heard this morning wasn't thunder, it was my stomach as the human saw fit to take me out BEFORE breakfast. However, I was a good pony and came home to a full feed bucket and a cuddle from a happy human. NOW I can have a day of lazy!

*

This morning:

Human: Wakey Wakey, rise and shine, it's time for a Lunge Match.

Me: What time do you call this?
Human: It's called beating the Horse Flies. Into the arena you go!
Me: I can't. I'm lame.
Human: Rubbish. You're just pretending.
Me: *develops a slight limp* no, really, I'm broken. You need to put me back in my field right now.
Human: Hmmm. Let me let you off the lunge a minute and see how you move round the arena.
Me: WAHOOOOO! FREEDOM! and jump out over the fence. Cheerio! *departs into long grass*

At this point, I'd have liked to say Game, Set and Match to me, but....

Human: You little toad (not her exact words but this is a family book). However, I have Christmas Mints here *rustles the wrapping*
Me: *from a distance* I hear rustling. This can only mean one thing - MINTS. Coming!!!!!
Human: ahaaaaa, GOTCHA. Back on the lunge and 40 minutes of work please.
Me: I can't, I'm worn out from jumping the fence.

No, I didn't get a mint either - the human ate the entire packet in front of me.

Phooey.

PONK

Incoming!!!!!!

This is the human celebrating the end of school with a bottle of something fizzy. I do think it was a bit rude to aim the cork in our direction. Not as rude as drinking it all first and THEN coming to feed us. Stuffing the haynets took an inordinately long time as the human was squiffy and kept missing and then she fell in the nettle patch while hanging mine. That sobered her up.

*

Well, this sucks. I have to share my paddock (and my haynet) with the brat while his is weeded. The human has already had to leave the cricket twice to break up the fisticuffs and consequently has missed something called a wicket which resulted in WORDS. Oops.

*

So, there are advantages to sharing with the Middle Sized Oik after all. I took everything back after he showed me how to itch open the gate and we had a pleasant afternoon lunching in the valley. The human arrived home from work to be greeted by distant burping and two Haflinger coloured Hot Air Balloons.
The gate is now quadruple tied with baler twine, lead ropes and a stirrup leather.
Whoops.

Well, I guess the quietness at the moment here at FP Towers proves one thing: that SFP is the naughty one and I am just easily led astray....

Sorry, did you just inhale your wine laughing?

*

The human isn't sure who to blame for the fence destruction and subsequent party across several fields but so far, I've come off worse with a severe schooling session and a newly zapped nose on the recharged fence. Phooey. Meanwhile, SFP has perfected the innocent look and has ended up having a cuddle. When is he going back to Pony School?

*

I have just been given an ASBO by the gamekeeper for scaring the pheasants in the cross country field. Whoops.

*

In the field this morning:
SFP: Play with me!
Me: No. I'm dozing.
SFP: Please play with me.
Me: NO. I'm still dozing.
SFP: *pulls at my rug a bit* Go on, play with me.
Me: NO!!!
SFP: *pulls a bit harder* pleeeeease?
Me: NOOOO!!!

SFP: Come on!!! We can GALLOP.
Me: I'M SLEEPING!!!

SFP then makes the basic error of trying to get one of my ears in his mouth. There is an unseemly tussle.

SFP: Mwffffff. MUMMMY!!!! He's sitting on me.
Me: ahhhh peace at last. Back to the doze....

You have to put these young upstarts in their rightful place you know.

*

New game: going up to a sleepy SFP (he had a sedation for the dentist) and pushing. He's all wobbly. I've been shouted at twice by the Human already.

*

Showing Granny my party trick of smooching the human when SFP decides he wants a go. The human now has stubble rash and a beard of mud. Mmmm, attractive...

*

Awoken from my slumber this morning by an approaching light akin to the Starship Enterprise which even made the local owls scarper. I retreat and snort a lot. It's the human and she has a new head torch. At least I now know when breakfast is approaching as do all the neighbours, passing aeroplanes and NASA...

Alerted by squeals, the human shines her super dooper torch out of the window to find 2 sets of eyes where there shouldn't be eyes.

Hello Human! We KNOW you've just had a bath and are all squeaky clean so do come out in the quagmire to try and lasso us and put us back in our field. You've brought reinforcements?

Bother. Best behaviour then *sigh*

And thus the pony party was ended with a subdued return to our paddock by a very irate human and the landlady. Note to self: don't squeal so much next time...

*

Honestly, I go out and do the hard work thing and when I get back, everyone's in bed. Sheesh.

Lovely woolly cuddles with the human (she has a nice fleecy dressing gown and I have a LOT of fur), right up to the moment I discovered she had mints in her pocket.
The fleecy dressing gown is now in the wash...

*

Luckily for me, the Oik wore the human out first and I was left to have a lazy in the field. In no way would I be trying to hide the fact I've lost a shoe. Not at all...

*

Chaos. And apparently all MY fault. The visiting Nephew has snitched on me, SFP is doing his best to look innocent and the elderly grey job is busy removing himself from the scene. Someone has eaten a month's worth of hay and the fencing covered all 8 acres.
Whoops.

*

Update
Alerted by yelling, out comes the human with her torch. SFP has escaped and the Nephew has snitched on him. I am in the correct place and looking innocent. See, it's not just me. The human says if we are not all in the correct place come daylight, we're all being made into rugs except the Nephew who is Mr Perfect.

I have work to do.

Noisily petitioning to come indoors as Storm Frank is whistling up my rug and making me very damp. And how dare the Met Office not call it Storm FP when they were dishing out names for our rubbish weather. I'm windy enough....

*

Hello Human! Happy New Year. No you can't ride - I've lost a shoe, sorry. The Oik? Good luck with that one - he's in a squealy mood and can currently be found doing the wall of death round the valley sides. You're going back to the sofa? Excellent plan.

I like 2016 so far #YearOfLazy

*

There has been an interesting shift in the balance of power here at FP Towers since the Nephew's visit. I am now Boss Pony and King of Everything I Survey (about 5 acres) and the Middle Sized Oik is now Boss Pony in Waiting and King of the Small Bog In The Corner. The Elderly Grey Job? Previously Boss Pony, he has been deposed and is now our Minion, only spoken to when one of us has an itch we can't reach. He's spending his days looking slightly anxious and his owner has had to build him a refuge so his breakfast isn't hoovered up by a large chestnut Dyson.
Field rules are simple - it's like living in a Minefield. Any hay is MINE, any grass is MINE and any carrots proffered by a

Human are MINE. I give it a week before the EGJ has moved fields...

*

There has been civil unrest in the night. The Elderly Grey Job is now King of The Paddock and Chief Hay Muncher. SFP and I have been reduced to mere underlings and are quietly arguing about who gets ownership of the Small Bog in the Corner. Hmph.

*

Human, Happy Birthday,
It's *cough cough* years and three,
A treat for you, I've not escaped,
(Don't mention SFP).
I'll try to be quite good today,
(You know I can't be perfect),
I'll guard the fence and pile of hay,
And keep the Oik in check.
So for your special day I'll give,
A bristly love filled hug,
A whiskery smooch from top to toe,
To cover you with mud

*

We see you. So when are we going to be allowed the other side of the fence then? What do you mean, never? Phooey.

MUMMY. I'm bored. Therefore I think it is only right that I create as much havoc as possible. I've got the Middle Sized Oik out of bed and we are going to do squealy laps of the valley* until the neighbours phone you to enquire if everything is ok. This'll teach you to watch rugby instead of come and play with us!!

* Sadly the Oik only lasted one lap before he went back to bed claiming a surfeit of dressage. However, the Elderly Grey Job was up for the challenge, mainly because I bit his bottom all the way round. I think he's on the phone to the human too...

*

Nope. We're both in bed and therefore can't be ridden. Sorry. What do you mean, get up? No Comprendo....

*

Hello Human. I see you've come down to the field for cuddles with a glass full of something clinky that looks suspiciously like a G&T with ice. You're celebrating the Middle Sized Oik being good??!!
snort
Well let me shed some hair into it so it's completely undrinkable. You're welcome.

*

Evening cuddles with the Human. She looks like a Yeti now

I have carefully made very, very sure that I am not this year's show pony by itching out precisely 9 inches of mane. It still elicited a sort of squeaky hyperventilation from the Human (especially as she'd been so careful with the rugs and everything over the winter and that bit of mane was looking quite good) but it's the Oik's go this year and I wanted to doubly make sure I couldn't be hauled out in reserve, especially as we still only have cold baths. As I now look like something that has gone through a hedge backwards, I'd count that as a result. Smirk.

*

Can I gallop? What do you mean, no?
Can I gallop now? What about now? Now? NOW? Ah phooey, I'm galloping anyway. Best of luck gathering your reins and putting the camera away at this speed....

*

The Human thought I was looking a bit skinny today (result!) so she left the gate open for me to have some grass while she rode the Oik. 40 minutes of wailing later they arrived back to discover that despite walking straight past it, I did not notice the open gate. The Human says that shows where the brains are in the field. Humph.

Too foggy to see the Super Moon here. However, due to a slight rug incident, there is a glorious Super Moon of a different nature happening at my tail end.... SFP says it's quite spectacular. The Human on the other hand says I am a disgrace and it's my own fault if my bum gets cold. Snigger.

*

Christmas Eve in the paddock:

Me: It's dark and the Human is late. I'm hungry.

SFP: Father Christmas will arrive before she does at this rate.

Me: But Hark! What is that yonder making its way through the mud?

SFP: Behold, for it is the Human bearing gifts from afar.

Me: But where is the star shining bright?

SFP: It probably has a flat battery.

Me: We had better go and check. AHHHHH she has carrots!

SFP: CHARGEEEEEEEE!

SPLATTTTTT

Human: ARGHHHHHHHH! Can't you at least TRY and be good on Christmas Eve of all days???

Me: Sorry. The Good just ran out....

Acknowledgements

As always, thank you to the thousands of FP fans out there who inspire me to keep posting his exploits and antics.

Sarah, for being a bad influence on the Human's gin habit and the lovely Nephew.

Emily and Hazel who continue to be a bad influence when it comes to Austrian puddings.

Tash and Kirsty for training the Scottish Oik to do as he's told instead of listening to me. It's no fun but at least the Human hasn't had a nervous breakdown.

And finally the nice doctors at Gloucestershire Royal Infirmary who screwed the Human back together. We're sending her back so you can unscrew her again next year....

#0100 - 181116 - C0 - 210/148/4 - PB - DID1656502